What I Li~~

Little Stars

KU-213-214

My Food

Liz Lennon

W

FRANKLIN WATTS
LONDON • SYDNEY

I like food!
I like to
eat lots of
different things.

I like spaghetti. It goes *slurp* into my mouth.

It's eight o'clock in the morning – time for breakfast.

My cereal goes **POP** when I pour the milk over it.

I like soldiers
with my egg.

Fluffy scrambled eggs,
are warm and tasty.

We're off to the supermarket. There is lots of food here!

I chose a new cereal.
I can't wait to try it.

I'm getting hungry.
It's time for lunch.

It's cold today.
Brrr!
Hot soup
warms me up.

We are helping Dad make sandwiches. Cheese and cucumber are my favourite.

I like to stack up sandwiches!

It's fun to
grow fruits
and vegetables.

In our garden we grow lettuce, tomatoes and carrots.

It's playtime! It's fun to run around, but now I am hungry again!

Crunch!
An apple is a
juicy snack.

It is six o'clock.
My stomach goes
rumble, rumble.
It's time for tea.

Dad tells me
to eat my
vegetables. Yuck!

Mum says
I should try
new foods.

I tried sweetcorn today, but I will never eat peas!

I like treats. Donuts are my favourite.

There are lots of treats at my birthday party. Crisps, cakes, sweets and ice cream.

It's hard to choose my favourite. Yum, yum!

About this book

Food is an important part of a young child's life and the aim of this book is to give you the opportunity to share and discuss different aspects of it. Looking at and talking about the pictures is a good starting point. Here are some ideas for further talking points:

Food routines The book is structured around the meals and snacks we have each day. Why do they think it's important to eat a good breakfast? Which is their favourite meal? When do they feel most hungry?

Where food comes from Talk about growing foods in the garden and relate it to farming and the food in the shops.

Making food Young children love to make food and, when they do so, are more likely to try new foods. Talk about the importance of keeping hands clean when preparing food. Although we can't see germs, we know they are there because they can make us sick.

Eating our vegetables Discuss which vegetables the child likes to eat. Which ways of cooking or serving vegetables do they like?

Trying new foods It is important to keep expanding young children's diet and encourage them to try new foods. You could set a challenge to try one new food a week.

Treats Treats, such as sweets, chocolate and cake, are okay occasionally but too many are bad for us. Discuss why.

First published in 2011
by Franklin Watts

Copyright © Franklin Watts 2011

Franklin Watts
338 Euston Road
London NW1 3BH

Franklin Watts Australia
Level 17/207 Kent Street
Sydney, NSW 2000

All rights reserved.

Dewey number: 641.3
ISBN: 978 1 4451 0466 9

Printed in China

Series Editor: Sarah Peutrill
Art Director: Jonathan Hair
Series Designer: Paul Cherrill
Picture Researcher: Diana Morris
Consultants: Karina Philip
and Deborah Cox

Franklin Watts is a division of
Hachette Children's Books,
an Hachette UK company.
www.hachette.co.uk

Every attempt has been made to
clear copyright. Should there be any
inadvertent omission please apply to
the publisher for rectification.

Picture credits: Alamy: Asia Images
20; Blend Images 19; Jeff Greenberg 2;
David Grossmann 16; Loisjoy Thurston
6. Istockphoto: Candy Box Photo 8;
Chris Fertnig 17; Joe Gough 7; Marcus
Lindstrom 21; Liza McCorkle 22; Olga
Nayashkova 13; Eduard Titov 15; Nicole
S. Young 10. Shutterstock: Noam
Armann 14; Gemenacom 10tr; Richard
Griffin 6cr; Larisa Lofitskaya front
cover, 12; Magone 4c; Monkey Business
Images 9, 18b; Neelia 11; Renata
Osinska 3; Bojan Pavlukovic 18t; Edyta
Pawlowska 4t; Katharina Wittfeld 1, 23.
Superstock: Design Pics 5.